PROJECT: STEAM

GOO MAKERS

KELLY MILNER HALLS

Rourke
Educational Media

rourkeeducationalmedia.com

Before & After Reading Activities

Before Reading:

Building Academic Vocabulary and Background Knowledge

Before reading a book, it is important to tap into what your child or students already know about the topic. This will help them develop their vocabulary, increase their reading comprehension, and make connections across the curriculum.

1. *Look at the cover of the book. What will this book be about?*
2. *What do you already know about the topic?*
3. *Let's study the Table of Contents. What will you learn about in the book's chapters?*
4. *What would you like to learn about this topic? Do you think you might learn about it from this book? Why or why not?*
5. *Use a reading journal to write about your knowledge of this topic. Record what you already know about the topic and what you hope to learn about the topic.*
6. *Read the book.*
7. *In your reading journal, record what you learned about the topic and your response to the book.*
8. *After reading the book complete the activities below.*

Content Area Vocabulary
Read the list. What do these words mean?

bacteria
borax
eruption
fiber
flexible
gelatin
hydrogen peroxide
Pyrex
yeast

After Reading:

Comprehension and Extension Activity

After reading the book, work on the following questions with your child or students in order to check their level of reading comprehension and content mastery.

1. *What happens when you mix water and cornstarch?* (Summarize)
2. *Why does adding extra gelatin to Jell-O mix change the consistency?* (Infer)
3. *What are magnets attracted to?* (Asking Questions)
4. *Do you use any of the ingredients in these experiments for other purposes at home or school?* (Text to Self Connection)
5. *What happens when you mix soap and water with a hand mixer?* (Asking Questions)

Extension Activity

Expose your goo to new conditions: open air, the freezer, or sunlight. Observe and journal about how the material changes. Consider whether or not those observations might apply to other common substances.

TABLE OF CONTENTS

LET'S GET GOOEY!

Science can get a little gooey—and foamy and slimy! These projects are a great way to get a bit messy while exploring the science of matter and its interactions. What happens when you mix different substances? You're about to find out!

Make sure you have adult permission or supervision. Now let's get gooey!

Cornstarch Super Goo

Gather:

1. mixing bowl

2. one box of cornstarch

3. one cup (240 milliliters) of water

4. rectangular cake pan

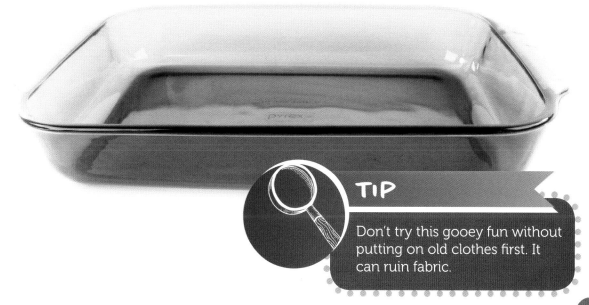

TIP

Don't try this gooey fun without putting on old clothes first. It can ruin fabric.

Do:

1. Add box of cornstarch to a mixing bowl.

2. Add water to the cornstarch. Mix with your hands.

3. Add a little more if the starch doesn't liquify right away.

4. Watch the goo slip and slide from your fingertips as a liquid.

5. Now pour the goo into a rectangular cake pan.

6. After a minute, slap the surface of the goo with your flattened hand. It's become a solid!

7. Now run your fingers through the mixture. It is a liquid again!

ALERT

Do not put the starch mixture down your sink drain. It will damage your pipes. When you finish playing, throw the slime in the garbage.

Observe:

When the water and cornstarch drips from your hands, the two ingredients are evenly mixed and they remain a liquid. When you pour the mix into the cake pan, the starch rises to the surface and separates from the water, making the top layer a solid. When you dig back into the goo, it mixes and once again drips from your fingertips.

Bubble Gum Goo

Gather:

1. 7.625 ounce (225 milliliter) bottle white school glue

2. mixing bowl

3. contact lens solution

4. one cup (240 grams) shaving cream

5. food coloring

6. one teaspoon (five milliliters) baking soda

7. four ounces (113 grams) Model Magic modeling compound

8. bubble gum flavoring drops

9. storage container

Do:

1. Pour glue into mixing bowl.

2. Add shaving cream.

3. Add pink food coloring.

4. Add bubble gum flavoring.

5. Add baking soda.

6. Add a splash of contact lens solution to begin thickening.

7. Add a little more contact lens solution if it's needed.

8. Mix with Model Magic modeling compound.

9. Enjoy your super smooth bubble gum scented slime!

10. Store in an airtight container.

ALERT

Your slime smells great, but do not eat it! Some ingredients could make you sick.

Observe:

Adding the shaving cream and Model Magic modeling compound transforms your slime into a super smooth dough that's fun to smell, twist, and shape.

Gooey Gummy Candy

Gather:

1. water

4. nonstick spray

2. **Pyrex** glass measuring cup

3. pot

5. three packets of unflavored **gelatin**

6. spoon

7. candy mold

8. one small package of Jell-O

9. stove (used with adult permission/supervision)

Do:

1. Bring a pot of water to a boil with an adult's help.

2. Pour one-third cup (80 milliliters) of water into the Pyrex glass measuring cup.

3. Slowly add three packets of unflavored gelatin. Stir briskly to keep it from clumping.

4. Once the gelatin is dissolved, add the Jell-O, Stir briskly.

5. Lower the Pyrex cup with your mixture inside into the pot of boiling water.

6. Stir as you heat your candy mixture.

7. Once the mixture is melted and thickened, remove from heat.

8. Your measuring cup shouldn't be too hot to touch.

9. Spray your candy mold with nonstick cooking spray.

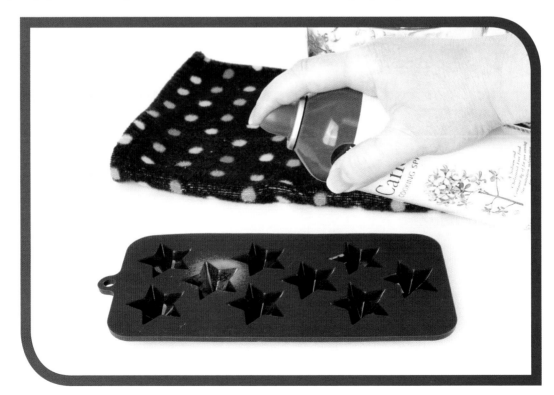

10. Carefully pour your candy mixture into the plastic shapes.

11. Allow the candy to cool and you'll have your own gummy candies.

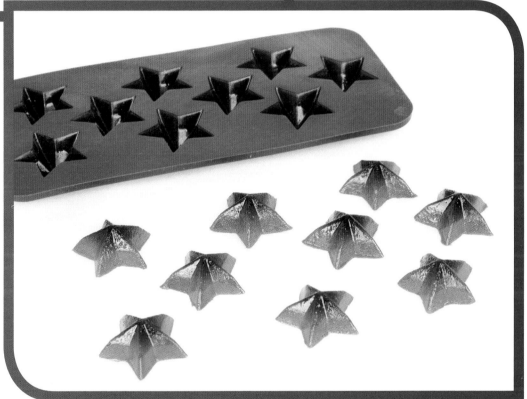

Observe:

By adding extra gelatin to traditional Jell-O mix, it forms a dryer candy, rather than a thick, refrigerated dessert.

Want to make sour gummy candy? Dip your gummies in a mixture of sugar and crystalized citric acid to make a tart alternative.

SLIME TIME

Hazy Crazy Slime

Gather:

1. 7.625 ounce (225 milliliter) bottle white school glue

2. two mixing bowls

3. food coloring

4. spoon

5. one tablespoon (15 milliliters) of **borax** laundry detergent, such as 20 Mule Team Borax

6. one cup (240 milliliters) warm water

7. airtight container

Do:

1. Pour all the glue in one mixing bowl.

2. Refill the glue bottle with water and shake.

3. Pour the water into the mixing bowl with the glue and stir.

4. Add food coloring and stir.

5. In the second mixing bowl, mix the detergent with the cup of warm water.

6. Slowly add the detergent and water mixture to the glue mixture. Don't add too much or your slime will turn rubbery.

ALERT

Do not eat your slime. Borax is toxic.

7. Mix thoroughly, first with a spoon, then with your hands until your slime is thick and squishy.

Observe:

The minerals in the detergent thicken the mixture and slows its usual hardening of the glue. As long as you keep your slime in a sealed container, it should last for up to two weeks.

Add strange, non-water-soluble items to your hazy slime to give it a new or spooky theme. Clear marbles look like spider eggs in colorful slime. Small pebbles or aquarium gravel gives it a weird texture.

Clear as Day-Z Slime

Gather:

1. 7.625 ounce (225 milliliter) bottle clear school glue

2. two mixing bowls

3. food coloring

4. glitter (consider using biodegradable)

5. spoon

6. one cup (240 milliliters) warm water

7. one tablespoon (15 milliliters) of borax laundry detergent, such as 20 Mule Team Borax

8. airtight container to store your slime

Do:

1. Pour all the glue in a mixing bowl.

2. Refill the glue bottle with water and shake.

3. Add the water to the mixing bowl with the glue.

4. Add food coloring and glitter to the mixing bowl.

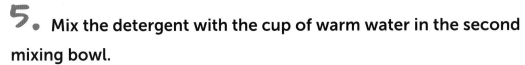

5. Mix the detergent with the cup of warm water in the second mixing bowl.

6. Slowly add the soap and water to glue mixture.

7. Mix thoroughly, first with a spoon, then with your hands until your slime is thick and consistent.

ALERT

Do not eat your slime. Borax is toxic.

Glitter makes clear, colorful slime look magical, but if you want slime that's gross, add plastic ants, spiders, or eyeballs to the mix.

Observe:

The minerals in the detergent thicken the mixture and slows the natural hardening of the glue. As long as you keep your slime in a sealed container when you're not playing with it, it should last for up to two weeks.

Magnetic Slime

Gather:

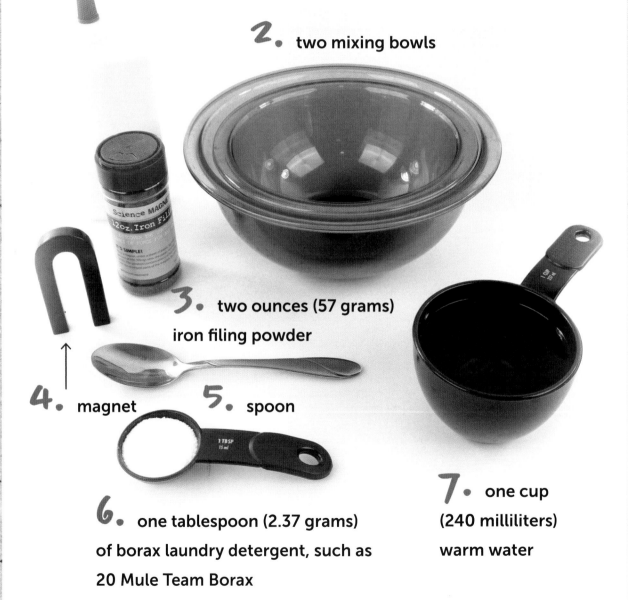

1. 7.625 ounce (225 milliliter) bottle white school glue

2. two mixing bowls

3. two ounces (57 grams) iron filing powder

4. magnet

5. spoon

6. one tablespoon (2.37 grams) of borax laundry detergent, such as 20 Mule Team Borax

7. one cup (240 milliliters) warm water

8. airtight container

Do:

1. Pour all the glue into a mixing bowl.

2. Fill empty glue bottle half full with fresh water and shake.

3. Mix the water with the glue.

4. Mix detergent with warm water in the second mixing bowl.

5. Add a bit of the water/detergent mix to your glue and stir slowly until it thickens. Don't add too much or the slime will turn rubbery.

6. Once you can easily handle the slime, add iron filing powder to the mixture.

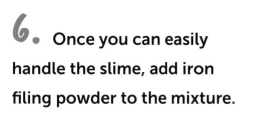

7. Use your hands to mix the iron filings with the white slime until it's mixed evenly.

ALERT

Do not eat your slime. Borax and iron filings are toxic. Do not swallow magnets, either.

8. Now see how your gooey slime reacts to a simple magnet!

9. Keep your finished slime in an airtight container for up to two weeks.

Try new experiments with your magnetic slime and magnets of different shapes and sizes.

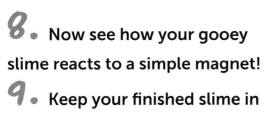

Observe:

Like your hazy and clear slime recipes, the detergent thickens the glue and water mixture. But it's the iron filings that really make it magic. Magnets are attracted to iron.

Funky Fiber Slime

Gather:

1. mixing bowl

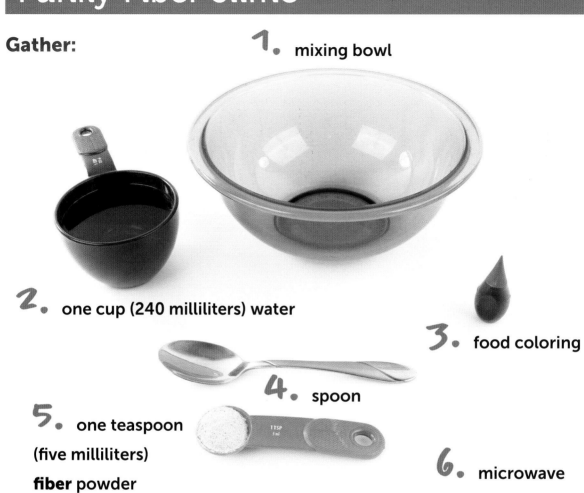

2. one cup (240 milliliters) water

3. food coloring

4. spoon

5. one teaspoon (five milliliters) **fiber** powder

6. microwave

Do:

1. Mix fiber powder and water in mixing bowl.

2. Add food coloring (optional).

3. Heat in microwave for two minutes.

4. Remove and stir well.

5. Heat in microwave for one more minute.

6. Refrigerate for 30 minutes.

7. Enjoy your gooey, non-toxic slime.

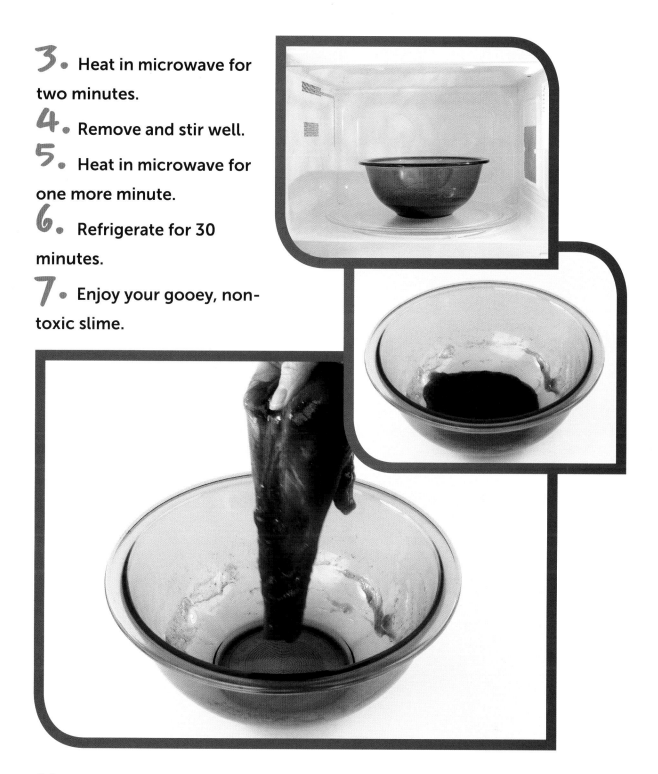

Observe:

The fiber powder bonds with the water to create a gooey, nontoxic slime. It is nontoxic, but it won't taste very good. And if you eat it, you may need to visit the toilet more often than normal that day. Fiber makes it easier to poop!

FOAM FUN

Rainbow Fun Foam

Gather:

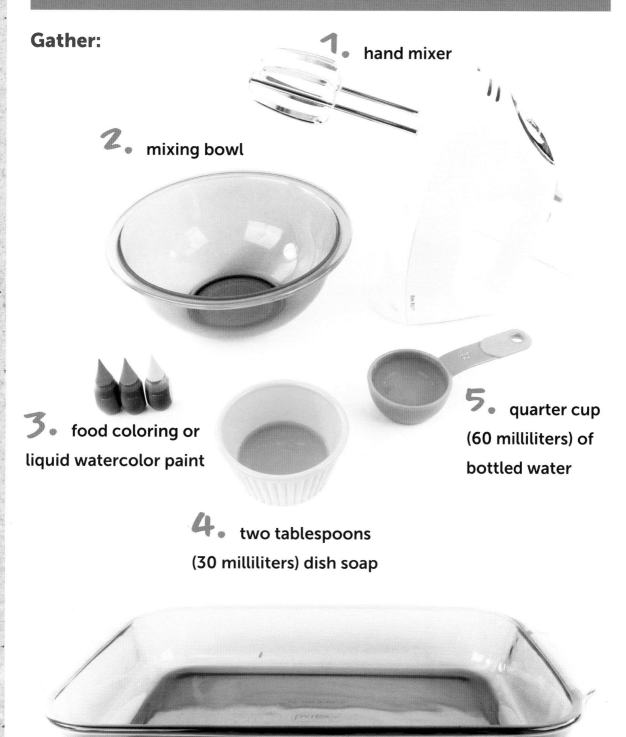

1. hand mixer

2. mixing bowl

3. food coloring or liquid watercolor paint

4. two tablespoons (30 milliliters) dish soap

5. quarter cup (60 milliliters) of bottled water

6. large cake pan

Do:

1. Put dish soap in the mixing bowl.

2. Add bottled water to the bowl.

3. Add a few drops of food coloring or liquid watercolor paint.

TIP

Food coloring stains, so wear old clothes if you use that to color your foam.

4. Mix with a hand mixer on the highest speed for one or two minutes.

5. When your foam can make stiff peaks, it's ready.

6. Move into the large cake pan.

7. Repeat the same steps to create more colors of foam.

8. Move those colors into the same cake pan.

9. Enjoy the sleek, slippery fun of your rainbow foam.

Observe:

By mixing soap and bottled water with a hand mixer, you infuse it with super tiny air bubbles—the higher the hand mixer speed, the tinier the bubbles.

TIP

Using bottled water instead of tap water makes the foam extra fluffy.

Hot Stuff Eruption Foam

Gather:

1. adult supervision!

2. medium-size plastic bottle with narrow neck

3. two and 1/4 teaspoons (7 grams) dry active **yeast**

4. two teaspoons (10 milliliters) very hot tap water

5. funnel

6. glitter (consider using biodegradable)

7. food coloring

8. half cup (120 milliliters) six percent **hydrogen peroxide**

9. two tablespoons (30 milliliters) of dish soap (Dawn works best)

10. spoon

TIP

Do this experiment outside so you can clean up the mess with your hose.

Do:

1. Combine hot water and yeast in a bowl and set it aside.

2. Add hydrogen peroxide, food coloring, dish soap, and glitter to the bottle.

3. Check the temperature of the bottle. It should be cool.

4. Using the funnel, add the yeast and water mixture to the bottle.

5. Check the temperature of the bottle. It should be hotter.

6. Step back and watch the hot foam **eruption**!

Observe:

When yeast is mixed in hot water, **bacteria** begins to rapidly grow. When the yeast combines with the hydrogen peroxide, the warming mixture expands and outgrows the space in the bottle. The steamy foam erupts in a fun and messy spectacle.

DELICIOUS DOUGH

Marshmallow Dough

Gather:

1. microwave-safe mixing bowl

2. one cup (50 grams) miniature marshmallows

3. food coloring

5. one teaspoon (4.35 grams) coconut oil

4. one and a half tablespoons (11.25 grams) cornstarch

6. microwave

Do:

1. Wash your hands well with soap. Dry them.

2. Put miniature marshmallows in a microwave-safe bowl.

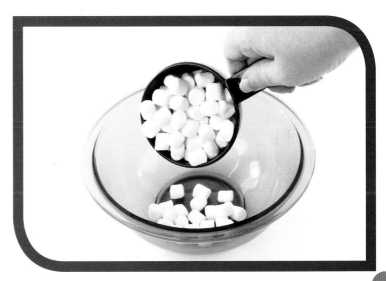

3. Heat in microwave for 30 seconds.

4. Add coconut oil to the melted marshmallows.

5. Add a few drops of food coloring.

6. Stir in cornstarch.

7. Knead with your fingers until you get a **flexible** dough.

8. If you keep it clean, you can eat your dough when you're finished with your squishy fun.

Observe:

When the sugar crystals bond with the cornstarch, the ingredients are transformed into a doughy consistency. Saving the dough is not recommended. Bacteria grow quickly in sugary substances.

Shape and Bake Bread Dough

Gather:

1. two mixing bowls

2. five cups (600 grams) flour

3. two cups (480 milliliters) warm water

4. two and a quarter teaspoons (7 grams) yeast

5. wire whisk

6. two tablespoons (25 grams) of sugar

7. one quarter cup (60 milliliters) vegetable oil

8. two teaspoons (10 milliliters) of salt

9. wooden spoon

10. small bowl of warm water

11. nonstick baking spray

12. cutting board

13. cookie sheet

14. extra flour for dusting

15. oven

Do:

1. Preheat oven to 350 degrees Fahrenheit (180 degrees Celsius).

2. Mix yeast, water, and sugar in large mixing bowl with a wire whisk.

3. Add oil and stir with whisk.

4. Mix remaining ingredients in a second mixing bowl.

5. Slowly add dry ingredients to wet bowl, using a wooden spoon.

6. Turn the dough onto a flour dusted cutting board.

7. Knead with clean hands for 10 minutes until dough is smooth.

8. Shape into the animals of your choice.

9. Use warm water as "glue" to attach one piece of dough to another.

10. Spray cookie sheet with nonstick baking spray.

11. Move dough shapes to cookie sheet.

12. Bake for 20 to 30 minutes.

13. Remove from oven and cool before eating.

GLOSSARY

bacteria (bak-TEER-ee-uh): microscopic, single-celled living things that exist everywhere.

borax (BOR-acks): a white, crystalline compound that naturally occurs as a mineral or is created from other minerals

eruption (i-RUHPT-shun): sudden, violent throwing out of lava, hot ash and steam

fiber (FYE-bur): a part of fruit, vegetables and grain that travels through the body to help with digestion

flexible (FLEK-suh-buhl): able to bend or change

gelatin (JEL-uh-tin): a clear substance made from animal bones and tissues used in making glue, Jell-O, and marshmallows

hydrogen peroxide (HYE-druh-juhn pur-OCK-side): an unstable combination of hydrogen and oxygen used as a whitening or cleansing tool

Pyrex (PIE-reks): heat and chemical-resistant glass

yeast (yeest): a yellow fungus used to make bread dough rise

INDEX

SHOW WHAT YOU KNOW

1. What purpose does the laundry detergent containing borax serve in these projects?
2. What makes foam fluffy?
3. Why are iron filings attracted to magnets?
4. Why is plastic glitter a better choice than metal flake glitter?
5. Where do bacteria grow quickly?

FURTHER READING

Ardley, Neil, *101 Great Science Experiments*, DK Children, 2014.

Heinecke, Liz, *Kitchen Science Lab for Kids: 52 Family Friendly Experiments from Around the House*, Quarry Books, 2014.

The Exploratorium, *Exploring Kitchen Science: 30 Edible Experiments and Kitchen Activities*, Weldon Owen, 2015.

ABOUT THE AUTHOR

Kelly Milner Halls is a writer who enjoys all things weird and wonderful. She explores life's mysteries in Spokane, Washington, where she lives with two daughters, too many cats, a Great Dane and a four-foot-long rock iguana named Gigantor.

www.rourkeeducationalmedia.com

PHOTO CREDITS: Cover & all pages: © creativelytara

Edited by: Keli Sipperley
Cover and Interior design by: Tara Raymo www.creativelytara.com

Library of Congress PCN Data

Goo Makers / Kelly Milner Halls
(Project: STEAM)
ISBN 978-1-64156-465-6 (hard cover)(alk. paper)
ISBN 978-1-64156-591-2 (soft cover)
ISBN 978-1-64156-707-7 (e-Book)
Library of Congress Control Number: 2018930491

Printed in the United States of America, North Mankato, Minnesota

Rourke Educational Media
Printed in the United States of America,
North Mankato, Minnesota